The

JOURNEY NEVER ENDS

How to Prepare a Spiritual Will

"Mary Petrosky's book is a treasury of Franciscan wisdom about how looking ahead to a world where I will no longer be present can help me live more deeply in *this* world, live more alive to the beauty of life around me, live more deeply into the mystery of the God who grounds my being and invites me to a life of love."

William R. Burrows
Research Professor of Missiology
New York Theological Seminary

"We have all been told to give away our lives, but few tell us how to give away our deaths just as generously. What a courageous and life-affirming idea! Mary Petrosky is your good guide here and in ways that you perhaps never imagined. One wonders why dozens of books have not been written on this very important subject."

Rev. Richard Rohr, O.F.M.
Author of *Falling Upward*

"This is a small spiritual oasis amid the expansive modern secular desert. The enlivening questions Mary Petrosky asks reminds me of ones posited by Abraham Joshua Heschel. The themes she puts forth call to mind Henri Nouwen and Joyce Rupp. However, the suggestions made on how to write a 'spiritual will' are guided by her own life—born of more than sixty years as a woman religious committed to prayer, honesty, authenticity, and of course as a Franciscan, compassionate service. On a quiet evening or a break during the week please enter the oasis she has provided for you. This oasis book will help you not to miss what could be the heart of the remainder of your life and to become more keenly aware of the particular gift you are to others."

Robert J. Wicks
Author of *Riding the Dragon*

"It is a joy to read Mary Petrosky's very accessible guide to planning a spiritual will. Her own religious life experience has shaped a beautiful volume with warm, elegant suggestions on how to organize the reader's plans for a prayerful legacy."

Anne H. McCormick
Trustee of the Thomas Merton Legacy Trust

The

JOURNEY NEVER ENDS

How to Prepare a Spiritual Will

MARY PETROSKY, F.M.M.

Foreword by Thomas Lynch

Afterword by F. Edward Coughlin, O.F.M.

AVE MARIA PRESS AVE Notre Dame, Indiana

To my parents Harry S. Petrosky and Loretta Linnemann Petrosky, who gave me life, faith, love, and spirit, I dedicate this book. Their faith and love continue to surround me.

CONTENTS

FOREWORD

It was at the Ninth Franciscan Forum a few years ago when I first met Mary Petrosky. The confab was held at a Jesuit university in Denver in June and organized around the subject of "Dying as a Franciscan: Approaching Our *Transitus* to Eternal Life and Accompanying Others on the Way to Theirs." Neither Jesuit nor Franciscan, religiously literate and religiously lapsed, I'd known a good few monks and nuns and Christian Brothers over the years and welcomed the opportunity to be part of a serious conversation on last things. I'd been a funeral director all of my adult life and written and read on mortality and mortuary arts and regarded the reverend clergy as fellow pilgrims in life's mysterious odysseys and undertakings.

    Sr. Mary was speaking just before lunch on "A Franciscan Spirituality of Dying," and after lunch, with another Franciscan, on "Transition and Loss at the End of Life." I was to finish off the afternoon with "Bereavement and Rituals of Mourning." Two friars were opening and closing the two-day forum on existentials and eschatologies, the sacred and the secular, the finite and funereal. Comfy with the lexicons, I was certain to get more from the adventures than I'd actually give.

I sought out Sr. Mary over lunch and learned she had spent a portion of her religious life in Papua New Guinea serving the people of that distant, difficult region of the South Pacific where my father had served during World War II with the US Marines. She was currently working with aging Franciscans in Manhattan.

She put me in mind of those desert ascetics from centuries ago who'd learned from desolation how to discern what to love and what to ignore, who played in a deeper end of the pool than most, and while I'd seen abject grief and no shortage of tragedy and heartbreak in the daily grind of my professional duties, Sr. Mary had wrestled with the answerless angels of theodicy in hers. And yet she maintained a lightness of heart that made her joyous with her lot in life, safe in her faith in God's abundant love and sufficient grace, undeserved and ever-present to the suffering bodies and souls of the world, and those who care for them, herself among them.

In a time when the prosperity gospel informs the body politic as well as the triumphalism that passes for religion, it is important to affirm the notions of redemptive suffering, salvific loss, and the letting go that gives us purchase. Mary Petrosky's work and writing bids us bequeath to those we love some of our gravid and lighthearted nature of being.

The reader of this slim volume of good tidings may have, as I had on first meeting Mary, the immediate sense of encountering a spiritual superior. I sensed it unambiguously, in ways that I can neither enunciate or deny. I'd experienced this before, on meeting a young pediatric oncologist, the niece of a dear friend; she's grown into a happy young wife and mother and medical director of a children's palliative care ward, a place of such acute grief and surpassing help-lessness that hearts were broken there every day. And I'd encountered it in the last weeks of my mother's slow death from cancer, at home, among her heart-wracked husband and their nine helpless children. She seemed to continue, as her body failed and her voice grew still, to grow in grace. The ineluctable gift of such encounters changes lives.

Among the things I had lamented in my remarks at the Franciscan Forum was the estrangement that mortuary fashions enforce between the living and the dead. The so-called "celebration of life," which has largely replaced the Christian funeral, is notable for the fact that everyone is welcome but the one who has died. The finger food is good; the talk is uplifting; the homiletics life-affirming; the music is suitable for the dentist's chair or roller rink and everyone is smiling except the corpse, which has been disappeared, most often for a fee by someone like me. What is worse, I told the assembled religious, whereas in the past I was accustomed to disposing of dead Methodists and Muslims, Catholics and Lutherans, Baptists and Reformed Jews, Episcopalians and various Calvinists—nowadays it was more bikers and bowlers, golfers and gardeners, birders and bass fishermen. The dead were defined and their memorial events designed not so much around what they'd hoped for or kept faith in, but what they did with their free time. To wit, their pastimes defined them more than their beliefs, their hobbies more than their hermeneutics.

The Journey Never Ends emboldens us to fix this, and to bear age, infirmity, sickness, and death, each in its unpredictable season, as imitations of the suffering by which we are, by faith, in fact redeemed.

Sr. Mary beckons us away from the trifling and idiosyncratic and toward the core of being, away from the accessories and toward our essential selves whence our legacy and true inheritance comes. *The Journey Never Ends* responds to the hunger, shared by all of us, to be known intimately and authentically, and serves as a reliable spiritual guide for fellow pilgrims making their way, generation after generation, to the ones we love; good orderly direction for the soul in search of home.

Thomas Lynch

Introduction
THE JOURNEY NEVER ENDS

I fell in love the first day of my sophomore year in college. It wasn't love for the professor, however, or any other person. The class was my first course in philosophy, and I fell in love with the weighty four questions that our professor, a Dominican priest, proposed to us that day:

Who am I?
Where did I come from?
Where am I going?
How do I get there?

He wrote them out on the blackboard and told us that the history of philosophy could be fashioned around attempts to answer those four questions. I sat in my chair completely enthralled. Soon, those questions defined so much of my life; they became, starting then and there, a lifelong search that I have continued to this day.

Decades later, I realize that this love affair of mine with questions had actually begun a year before college, during my senior year in high school at a Catholic girls' academy in Cincinnati, Ohio. It was then, while leisurely searching in the school library's philosophy section (not knowing much about the subject, but already drawn to it), that I came across a book by a man named Boethius. What a name! There was no one on my block named Boethius. The book was titled, *The Consolation of Philosophy*.[1]

I knew nothing about Boethius or his book back then, but I began browsing through it until I came upon a few pages about the emptiness of searching for notoriety, for popularity, or for worldly success. This medieval author recognized long ago that rarely, if ever, is anyone actually successful at becoming universally known, respected, or loved. In other words, as he explained, the pursuits themselves almost always end in failure! I do not have the exact quotation at hand now as I write this to you, but I remember well how those thoughts placed my life into a new orbit.

Being a teenager at the time, and a high school senior, I was understandably somewhat preoccupied at that time with what Boethius was warning against: worldly notions of success. I was considering what I would and should do with my life, knowing that whatever it was to be, I wanted to be successful. Don't we all feel that way at that age? Thank God, however, my teachers and my parents reinforced Boethius's message in my life; they made it clear that any success I would achieve would come by using what God's gifts were to me to better the lives of others.

I was raised Christian from my earliest days, with deep down Catholic roots. I'm thankful for that. Still, looking back, I recognize that from then until now, (I'm now in my mid-eighties), I would have described myself as a natural seeker and searcher. In other words, the looking and the questioning have never stopped, even though I know now pretty clearly where I am going!

Boethius's *Consolation of Philosophy* not only opened my mind, but helped direct my soul. It helped to deepen my questioning and my searching into a vocational choice. Reading Boethius helped to lead me to choose religious life from seeds that had been planted in me by a family firmly rooted in the Catholic Church. While still a young person, I knew that I wanted to live in service to God, the Church, and to others. Like a few of the women saints whom I've known and loved (St. Teresa of Avila, for instance), I was willing and maybe even longing for martyrdom, in order to show just how serious I was.

I have been a member of the Franciscan Missionaries of Mary for sixty-five years now, and as a member of an International Missionary Institute, I've had the privilege of serving in several countries on other continents, as well as here in the United States, in cities and rural areas. I haven't had notoriety, or the kind of success that makes the newspapers. And I haven't been universally loved, just as Boethius predicted that I wouldn't. Those things have not been mine to possess; nor have they been my goals. I am a follower of St. Francis of Assisi, and so my goal has long been, and grows ever deeper: to find God in all things and in all people.

Those original four questions from my sophomore year in college inspired and haunted me over all of the years from then until now. I ponder them still, even though I am mostly at peace now with my answers. Also, in the sunset of my life, those four questions have led me to an essential fifth one. The fifth is not as deep or searching as the four were and are, but it is now a most personal and immediate question for me. Life teaches that what seems personal, most often, is also universal. The fifth question is:

What do I want to leave behind?

Is there something about me, about my life right now that could encourage, challenge, or maybe even bring a smile, a laugh, or a prayer to the lives of others? Is there something of my life at present that might inspire, amuse, or challenge my loved ones, friends, coworkers, neighbors, and in so doing help them to recognize that I found purpose and meaning? How did they come to define my life?

Or, could it be that I haven't yet begun to find—or build, or create—the contribution that is uniquely me and mine in this world?

Where and how will I make my mark on life?

Perhaps you are here asking the same things. If you are, then we're in this together, and you're in the right place. As long as we are alive, our spiritual growth continues, and there is no time better than now to remind yourself who you are and who you want to be. When your life comes to an end, what do *you* want to leave behind for others? More importantly, ask yourself now: Who do *you* want to be?

If you would like to reflect on what you want your loved ones to remember about what you consider the *core of your being*, then this is the book for you.

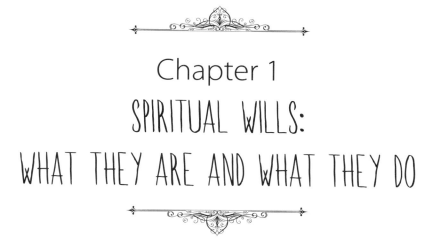

Chapter 1
SPIRITUAL WILLS:
WHAT THEY ARE AND WHAT THEY DO

What exactly is a spiritual will? It is easier to begin by telling you what it is not.

A spiritual will is not a last will and testament, the best-known form of communicating with loved ones after a death in most Western cultures. Heirs sometimes wait in anticipation of hearing someone's last will and testament in order to receive money, property, heirloom jewelry, or other valuables that they've been hoping to acquire. This book is something different.

It is not necessary to wait until Social Security age to think about your legal will, and yet, most people wait until late in life to prepare one. Please don't make that mistake when it comes to a spiritual will. Why? Because this is too important to postpone.

Throughout our adult lives, we need to think seriously about life and what our individual lives mean. Who are we and who do we want to be? We need to remember, direct (or redirect), and plan now in order to make the contribution we want to make to our family, our friends, our profession, our neighborhood, our country, the world. The reflections we focus on will help us to decide what it means to live now and into the future.

We are choosing what we want to experience more of, or more deeply: life, love, family, faith, career, ministry—the imprint that we will make. It is this that will be the material for what we want to be remembered by, for, and as. All of this is so much more important than a legal will!

Begin to figure this out now and the process will help you to direct what you do and who you will become in the decades to come. Writing a spiritual will is a way of discerning what is of enough value to you to dedicate your vision, your gifts, and your energy to—so that, by the time you get to my age, you will be proud of the life you have lived. You will have created, with God's help, the life that you want to be remembered for. You will be able to look back on what you wrote in this spiritual will and say: I did it!

A spiritual will is also about what you have learned: perhaps values formed by love, friendship, service, success, failure, relationships, integrity, as well as your personal moral tenor. Expressed in your unique, personal voice—not in legalese—a spiritual will concerns who you are and who you have become over the course of your life: your values, interests, experiences, relationships, and perhaps your faith. Much more than an accounting of your earnings, your stuff, a spiritual will articulates your deepest values for your loved ones to remember you by.

This Is Not a New Idea

Our Jewish brothers and sisters are often encouraged to write what is called in Jewish moral teaching, an ethical will. Rabbi Jack Riemer and Dr. Nathaniel Stampfer have described ethical wills as containing "the desire to bequeath to their descendants an instructive account of the ideals and *midot* (traits, measures of refinement) closest to their hearts."[2] The purpose is to transmit one's personal reflection on what it has meant to live life as a Jew, and on the motivating values and events in one's life experience. Riemer and Stampfer make clear that ethical wills have their roots in the Bible and the Talmud.

The purpose of the book you are holding now is to create something similar to an ethical will, but from the specific understanding of your spiritual life and practice, reflecting on how your spirituality is living out of, and based upon, your faith and interests, the use of your gifts, and the endeavors, accomplishments, perhaps even failures, that have marked your life. A spiritual will must have roots in the spiritual tradition of your identity. It is like an ethical will, deeply humanitarian, moral, and intellectual, but it is also more than that.

Who Is This For?

Many people today no longer identify as belonging to an established church or system of religious belief, but define themselves as broadly "spiritual." Being spiritual can mean many things, but usually a spirituality can be recognized by one's activities. These non-church-going activities might include sports or body work (yoga, tai chi, etc.); artistic, musical, or literary interests; vocational accomplishments; or independent spiritual endeavors such as Eastern and Western forms of prayer, meditation, and other practices.

You who are broadly spiritual can benefit from creating a spiritual will just as much as the person who is involved in an organized faith. *All* people, in my experience, find creating a spiritual will to be a deeply reflective experience. While eulogies are generally another person's remembrance of you (which, by the way, you never get to hear!), creating a spiritual will is a way that you define yourself. In this way, crafting your own spiritual will can be similar to writing your own eulogy! Creating one, now, might even affect the way that you live the rest of your life—as you "hear" yourself say what is most important to you.

In a spiritual will we describe what is important to us, and what is worthy of being remembered, even imitated, from our lives. The value of going through this process is that you can choose what you feel reflects not only your actions and deeds, but your soul. A spiritual will is a summary of your unique reflections about life and living from the perspective of the core beliefs and principles that have given meaning to your life.

In order to get started, begin by asking yourself some basic questions. Remember, for instance, those first two questions from my philosophy professor:

Who am I?
Where did I come from?

These are good launching pads. Ponder your answers to them, first, from a familial point of view. What did your family teach you that you have tried to embody? Most of us can go back in memory, as well as to written and photographic records, at least to our grandparents, and even sometimes to our great-grandparents, but not much further unless we do a real ancestry search. Ancestry studies can take us back many more generations to other times, countries, cultures, economies, and the challenges which previous generations faced.

What have previous generations learned and passed on to you? Because of changing times, many of the things learned in and from previous generations may no longer be relevant, but the values and wisdom with which the decisions were made, as well as the consequences of those decisions, are worth reflecting upon. What was important to them, in their generation, which transcends time and place? Some examples might be love of family, beauty around them, opportunities for education and employment, a community with mutual compatible interests, particular beliefs. Or, perhaps, the opposites of these! Pause and consider these things as you ponder "Who am I?" and "Where did I come from?"

What one generation learns, another may ignore, reject, forget, or even misunderstand.[3] The wisdom of some of the past generations' choices, in their time, may not be relevant in today's world, but certainly something was learned, either positive or negative. This process will probably make you wish that your grandparents, great-grandparents, and beyond had written spiritual wills for you! This is one of the reasons why you are going through the process to create one now: to leave behind for your future generations.

There is an ongoing challenge for the present to learn from the past. Generations that have come before us still live in our souls and sometimes in our hearts. They are actually part of our DNA. When we can join time and space to the here and now we may discover the wisdom, or perhaps the folly, of our forebears. It is good to pass on to the next generation the wisdom and the truths that we have come to know, as well as the lessons, joys, and sorrows that have come to make us who we are.

Record your answers to those first two questions in chapter 5 (pages 51–62). This is where you will compose your spiritual will. You may also download a pdf or Word document at www.avemariapress. com/myspiritualwill.

As we go on to the next steps, keep also in mind that writing a spiritual will is one means of discovering yourself, and the process presupposes and even demands a true and honest knowledge of who you are and where you have come from. This won't work if you are not willing to be honest.

Edgar Albert Guest (1881–1959) helped all of us reflect on our true selves when he wrote this searching poem, titled "Myself":

I have to live with myself and so
I want to be fit for myself to know.
I want to be able as days go by,
Always to look myself straight in the eye;
I don't want to stand with the setting sun
And hate myself for the things I've done
I don't want to keep on a closet shelf
A lot of secrets about myself
And fool myself as I come and go
Into thinking no one else will ever know
The kind of person I really am,
I don't want to dress up myself in sham,
I want to go out with my head erect
I want to deserve all men's respect;
But here in the struggle for fame and wealth
I want to be able to like myself.
I don't want to look at myself and know that
I am bluster and bluff and empty show.
I never can hide myself from me;
I see what others may never see;
I know what others may never know,
I never can fool myself and so,
Whatever happens I want to be
Self-respecting and conscience free.[4]

Self-knowledge is what the philosophers would call a *sine qua non*, or "absolute condition," for writing a spiritual will. Transparency is key!

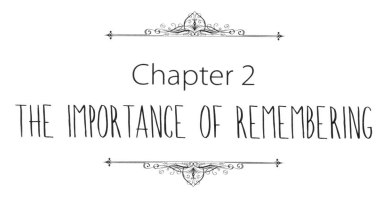

Chapter 2
THE IMPORTANCE OF REMEMBERING

Writing a spiritual will is about naming who we are at our core. How do I go about identifying what I consider to be my core—what the Trappist monk Thomas Merton called my "true self," rather than my "false self"? In his book, *New Seeds of Contemplation*, Merton wrote,

> Every one of us is shadowed by an illusory person: a false self. We are not very good at recognizing illusions, least of all the ones we cherish about ourselves.
>
> Contemplation is not and cannot be a function of this external self. There is an irreducible opposition be-tween the deep transcendent self that awakens only in contemplation, and the superficial, external self which we commonly identify with the first person singular.
>
> Our reality, our true self, is hidden in what appears to us to be nothingness. . . . We can rise above this unreality and recover our hidden reality.

God Himself begins to live in me not only as my Creator but as my other and true self.[5]

In other words, together with God, we each find that true self
inside of us. And it is from the core of our true self that we will see
what identifies who we really are.

In his book, *And Now I See*, Bishop Robert Barron offers a wider
perspective on Merton's approach to finding the true self. Bishop
Barron explains that Merton felt his life was a battleground between
conflicting interests, warring tendencies, and mutually conflicting
"selves." Merton's true life was an awakening to the true "I," the Christ
living in him, while dying to the vaporous and destructive ego created by fear. These were the two selves battling within him.[6]

Something similar probably takes place in each of us. You may be
aware of who you are, and also of your gifts, but perhaps you haven't
reflected sufficiently in order to find the words that describe this well.
This may be because you have not yet gotten to know, or identify, your
"true self" enough to own it.

As we all age, the desire to be known for who we really are
becomes increasingly more important. Likewise, leaving this earth
without friends and loved ones knowing the real you can leave a vac-
uum in them—and in you—and we realize this increasingly, too, the
older we become.

As you've now begun to ponder this process in a variety of
ways, you have surely also reflected on family members, friends,
and colleagues who have died before you. Maybe you've already felt
some regret as to how little you knew them. Maybe you've experienced feelings of sadness on occasions when others were able to
speak about your family members or friends, mentioning their gifts,
their humor, what pleased or distressed them, that you did not know
firsthand. Perhaps you've wished that you could have known more

before they died. That is just one reason why remembering can be very important—not only for us personally, but for those who are close to us.

There's Something Distinctively Catholic about Remembering

The act of remembering is essential to the way we Catholics view the world and understand our faith.

Most Catholics who have a little bit of theological background are aware that the highlight of the Mass is the Liturgy of the Eucharist. We all know the Eucharistic Prayer, a prayer of thanksgiving and sanctification. "Lift up your hearts," the priest says to the congregation. "We lift them up to the Lord," we say. This leads to the consecration, when, by means of repeating the words and actions of Christ, the sacrifice is effected which Christ himself instituted during the Last Supper. Always our exemplar, Jesus Christ left us more than a spiritual will when he shared the bread and wine at the Last Supper. It was then and there that he spoke these famous words: "Do this in remembrance of me" (Lk 22:19). Repeating these words accompanies the actual consecration of the elements of bread and wine.

All of this (and more) is liturgically followed by what is called *anamnesis*. In the words of the US Conference of Catholic Bishops, the anamnesis is the way

> by which the Church, fulfilling the command that she received from Christ the Lord through the Apostles, celebrates the memorial of Christ, recalling especially his blessed Passion, glorious Resurrection, and Ascension into heaven. The oblation, by which, in this very memorial, the Church, in particular that gathered here and now, offers the unblemished sacrificial Victim in the Holy Spirit to the

Father. The Church's intention, indeed, is that the faithful not only offer this unblemished sacrificial Victim but also learn to offer their very selves, and so day by day to be brought, through the mediation of Christ, into unity with God and with each other, so that God may at last be all in all.[7]

The word *anamnesis* is used in both medicine and in theology. It has both Greek and Latin roots. In medicine, anamnesis describes the physician's search into the complete case history of the patient. For our purposes in theology and liturgy, anamnesis is the deep recollection and reflecting on all that has led up to the words the priest says as he elevates the bread and then the wine: "Do this in remembrance of me." What was mere bread and wine is now the Body and Blood of Jesus Christ.

In the pre–Vatican II liturgy, and in some churches still today, these actions are accompanied with the server (acolyte) ringing small bells, alerting the faithful to this momentous event, now present on the altar in front of them. Unfortunately, I think that some Catholics may mistakenly think that the moment of consecration, and at the spoken words, "Do this in remembrance of me," is only a memory of someone who isn't there, not a participation in an ongoing mystery of the Risen Christ.

Anamnesis is a key concept in liturgical theology. In worship, the faithful recall God's saving deeds. These include the events both in the Old Testament, and particularly, in the New Testament. This memorial aspect is not just a passive process but one through which the Christian can actually enter into the Paschal Mystery, our salvation history. In 1 Corinthians 11:23–26, we read:

> For I received from the Lord what I also handed on to you, that the Lord Jesus, on the night he was handed over, took

bread, and after he had given thanks, broke it and said, "This is my body that is for you. Do this in remembrance of me." In the same way, also the cup, after supper, saying, "This cup is the new covenant in my blood. Do this, as often as you drink it, in remembrance of me." For as often as you eat this bread and drink the cup, you proclaim the death of the Lord until he comes.

And in the Old Testament, we recall Isaiah 40:8: "Though the grass withers and the flower wilts, the word of our God stands forever!"

It is at the Mass, listening to the words spoken by the priest at the offertory and the consecration, that we hear again and experience how God sent his Son to show us the way. Every time we hear those words, "Do this in remembrance of me," we are invited to enter fully into a life of transformation through imitation of all that we know of Christ's life on earth.

Reflecting again on Thomas Merton's language, to be my "true self" means to engage daily in a kind of transformation. I believe that we do this through a deeper understanding of anamnesis: remembering. Remembering is how we can find help in discovering our true self. Guided by Holy Scripture, we begin to discover that the true self is most easily found in service to others, in letting the false self be displaced, in abandoning the search for the "ideal," and instead embracing the cross. Christ gave us this example when he walked upon our earth and encountered the human condition in situations calling forth both the joys and sorrows of being human.

Applying Anamnesis in Your Life

In light of remembering the sacrifice of Jesus each time we attend Mass, we can consider our own lives and begin to discern the gifts God has given us and the moments in which God has touched our lives.

A good place to start may be to ask, "What is it that I have I received from the Lord? What has God given to me?" Think of the powerful memories of joy, sorrow, pain (physical or psychological) in your life. Recall the peak experiences that have marked your life in body, mind, and spirit. As you review your life's most significant events, reflect on the ways that you were changed, positively or negatively, always keeping in mind God's constant presence and care. Considering our lives in the context of a relationship with God, who is always calling us to grow, can allow us to see significance and even grace in events that might otherwise seem devastating and even meaningless.

Scripture may also be a rich source of insight. Our own personal responses to the Bible in Mass or scripture are clues that the living Word of God is speaking to us. As the letter to the Hebrews tells us, "Indeed, the word of God is living and effective, sharper than any two-edged sword, penetrating even between soul and spirit, joints and marrow, and able to discern reflections and thoughts of the heart" (Heb 4:12).

Think about biblical verses and phrases that struck you when you heard or read them, changing your perspective and framing things in a new way. Perhaps these passages remained in your heart over the years, forming and informing your thoughts and coming to mind along life's journey.

As we encounter the living Word in scripture, our true self begins to emerge. The Gospels are an inexhaustible source of encounter with God. Ask yourself, "What is my favorite Gospel story about Jesus?" Perhaps there is a healing story of Jesus which has particularly moved you to the point of wishing to imitate, as much as possible, Jesus' encounter with the subject of the story. Recall the story and where you were when you heard or read it. What was going on in your life at the time? Were you aware of being at a crossroads, searching for guidance, or otherwise unsure how to proceed? Ask yourself, "Have I allowed myself to live out this story in any big or small ways in my life?" For example, when Jesus ministers to the lepers of his day, I find myself reflecting on the "lepers" we meet on our streets today: homeless, immigrants, Muslims, prisoners, gays and lesbians, prostitutes. The list can go on and on. Our reaction and approach to these situations help us identify our true self, the self we want to present in a spiritual will.

When at the Communion time we are invited to receive the Body and Blood of Jesus in the appearance of bread and wine, we are receiving a live body. We have Jesus within us, real food for the soul. He is now part of us. May he be our true self when we choose what it is that we want to write as our gift to others.

Simply put, anamnesis can be an instrument to help the writer of a spiritual will to clarify what they would like others to remember about their life, values, and faith. This might include a familial trait recognized or discovered, or a personal one developed consciously by you over the course of a lifetime. It might be a treasured word of Holy Scripture, passed down to you by one of your parents, or, more simply, a gesture of kindness, or a familiar Catholic devotion. Just as we sing in that great Catholic hymn:

> We remember how you loved us to your death,
> and still we celebrate, for you are with us here;
> and we believe that we will see you when you come in your
>   glory, Lord.
> We remember, we celebrate, we believe.[8]

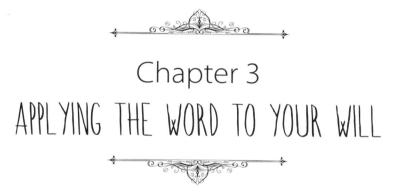

Chapter 3
APPLYING THE WORD TO YOUR WILL

Writers love words—just as much as readers do! As we all know, avid readers sometimes come to almost worship those words which, when read, form imaginary pictures, sometimes affecting their sight, smell, touch, and especially, their imagination. These are the occasions when we become "lost" in a book because we love it so much. Have you ever not wanted to turn the last page of a book, because you have "fallen in love" with the character and their story? Words can—in very real ways—"become flesh"!

The theology which underpins the writing of a spiritual will could well be an example of the words you choose becoming flesh for the people to whom you address your spiritual will. Words do have a transformative value and power.

The words you use should be carefully and reflectively chosen for the various people you may wish to address, and you may wish to choose to address different individuals in different ways.

The American poet Emily Dickinson loved words ardently. Her numbered poem 1651 begins:

> A Word made Flesh is seldom
> And tremblingly partook . . .

The second stanza is particularly appropriate for our purposes:

> A Word that breathes distinctly
> Has not the power to die
> Cohesive as the Spirit
> It may expire if He—
> "Made flesh and dwelt among us"
> Could condescension be
> Like this consent of Language
> This loved Philology.[9]

The words you want to choose in writing your spiritual will demand prayer and much thought. The writing may be a holy exercise. The writer of a legal will takes time to consider the distribution of his or her estate, and seeks advice as they prepare their document. If you are serious about what you want to leave of yourself to another, taking time to pray and to ponder on what you want others to know about you, and remember about you, can be the focus of some deep reflection. Some may even want to make it the focus of a weekend retreat—and/or a group study. (Refer to the back of this book for guidance.)

Sometimes our circle of friends or close family members can contribute to our reflection. Those with whom we have shared the most often have real insights into who we really are and can contribute unique words to describe us. To them, our predominant features, assets, or even our irritating idiosyncrasies are abundantly clear! What gives joy, as well as what irritates us, even angers us, reflected from a loved one, can give much insight into our values and our focus in life. It may be something you might not even have fully appreciated without the words of a friend.

I suggest ten principles, which I have used for decades with people whom I've counseled through this process. Keep these guidelines in mind as you reflect deeply upon what you want to write to others as either a summary of who you are, or who you are setting out to become, with God's help.

Ten Principles to Help Guide You in Writing a Spiritual Will

1. "God is love, and whoever remains in love remains in God and God in him" (1 Jn 4:16). It is absolutely necessary to believe, if not in God as he is traditionally described or defined, then in Power or Spirit (God has many names, after all!), and at the very least, something that is bigger and better than yourself. It is necessary to believe in the existence of goodness and love, both outside and inside of yourself. It is because of this goodness, both in you and outside of you, that you have been prompted to pass on some of what you have experienced in life and relationships to others.

2. Whatever you write must be thoroughly honest, genuine, and transparent. Always keep in mind how frequently and how easily we can fool ourselves, or even be in denial about some of the negatives inside of us.

3. The quality of your relationships to family and friends, both positive and negative, and what you have learned from them, are good areas to draw from as you name the values you have developed.

4.   Your hopes and dreams, realized and/or discovered to be unattainable so far in your life, can also provide profound areas of reflection.

5.   Awareness and love of mother earth—all of creation—can feed the choices you will make.

6.   Never forget that your sufferings and failures and what you have learned from them can be valuable "gifts" to others. Write about those, too.

7.   Your travels, at home and abroad, introducing you to a world you could never have imagined, have acquainted you with beauty and challenge and left lasting memories.

8.   The people of other races, cultures, and beliefs have surely opened you to many discoveries about them and yourself. Be sure to reflect on those.

9.   May "the eyes (and ears) of your hearts be enlightened, that you may know what is the hope that belongs to his call, what are the riches of glory in his inheritance among the holy ones" (Eph 1:18). Recognize and remember what good and not-so-good challenges have marked your life and brought you to this reflection.

10. Writing a spiritual will can be a sharing in the Communion of Saints. It is a strengthening and partaking of the spiritual as well as human bonds between members of the Church in heaven and on earth, united through grace, prayer, and good works.

Memento Mori, or Think About Your Death

The Communion of Saints reminds each of us to value our life, in part, by considering our death.

Each time I visit a cemetery and pass rows and rows of tombstones, attempting to find my family's plot, I am much more conscious of the dash between dates. This journey on earth goes so very quickly!

A popular poem called "The Dash," written by Linda Ellis, speaks in verse of what is truly significant about "the dash," the hyphen between the date of birth and the date of death. She explains that the dash represents all that the person was and did while on earth. I can't help but think about the lives, the loves, the interests, the challenges, the achievements and possibly the failures and the joys of each one resting under each particular marker as I walk through a cemetery.

One life may have been full of activities, accomplishments, loves, joys, and sorrows. Another life may have been colorless for activity and accomplishments that merit writing about, but rich in relationships and devotion to family. Many people I have known have lived lives that are unknown to the world at large, but are of huge significance to their family.

The tombstones or markers usually leave nothing more for another to know than the statistics, the date of birth and the date of death. Oh, how much is missing! Obituary notices in our newspapers give little more than one or two small paragraphs about the deceased, and may name the survivors to the last generation.

Some university courses relating to death and dying ask each student to write his or her obituary. It can be a very reflective exercise, even though it is a requirement. Whenever you do this, under whatever circumstances, writing your spiritual will can be of value to yourself as well as to those to whom you address it. The task invites you to engage in both a mental and spiritual journey into yourself. The result of the journey will help you answer the question, *Who am I?* and then maybe enter into *Where am I going?* You may even enter into the territory of *Where have I gone?* and *How did I get there?*

If you are in your thirties, forties, fifties, or maybe even sixties, you may feel that writing a spiritual will is something to do in the future, but not just yet, I would suggest that you nevertheless begin now by purchasing a journal (or starting a document on your laptop) and begin to jot down notes of what you want to remember to include. Sometimes ideas will come to you slowly and sometimes suddenly.

As you jot down these notes, your spiritual will begins to take shape. And I hope—as you begin the process—that you'll see its benefits in your life right now. A spiritual will is not something that's only for those of us who are statistically more likely to die in the near future!

A person of any age can begin to do this, but I have discovered that until one is older, or possibly facing a serious illness in midlife, one is not particularly thinking about dying and death, but mostly about living, and living life to the full. By doing this now, you are beginning to identify what is attracting you and is important to you, giving new meaning and depth not only to your life but also to the lives of others around you. These sometimes random but significant thoughts and reflections will provide material for writing the will when you feel you are ready to compose your very personal legacy.

It is really never too early to begin to think about this. When a child is born, one of the first things the parents consider is, if something should happen to them, to whom would they want to leave/ entrust their child/children.

The ten principles written above can help you focus, beginning to discover those things, those people, ministries, work, places, and even more important, faith and relationships which may begin to challenge or inspire you to see things in a new way, more deeply, or in a different light. Giving more thought to the important aspects of your life, your relationships, your interests, and identifying what is beginning to draw you, you are preparing to choose what will be the focus of not only your life, and also of your person, but of your soul!

The synthesis of all these aspects will define the true you, the self you want to leave behind as a legacy.

In *Final Harvest*, a book that collects and introduces Emily Dickinson's poetry, editor Thomas H. Johnson comments that Emily was, most of all, through her poems, asking if "there is any act, more blessed than the divine descent, the voluntary stooping to immanence, to reach the ear and the heart of the creature?"[10] Could there be anything more blessed or important to bring the word to life in our lives? Thoughts deeply processed and expressed can have sacramental value and can be life-giving as well as life-changing, maybe even transformative to another, as they have been for you. If well chosen, your words will give life to others, inspiring and motivating them. They will do that for you, too. Just as the words in the anamnesis, particularly, "Do this in remembrance of me," not only recall life but have the capacity to pass on life, your words have the power to do the same.

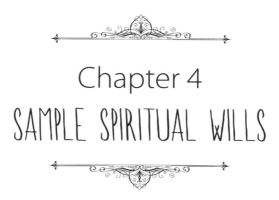

Chapter 4
SAMPLE SPIRITUAL WILLS

Another important consideration is the addressee of the spiritual will. That question can have a variety of answers and none is best. Your answer will really be up to you, after having thought about the people in your life. You may be considering addressees who are friends, or family, people from the neighborhood, work colleagues, and people whom you've known in faraway places. Maybe you even have in mind someone whom you sat next to on a plane, train, or bus, or whom you met on some other unique occasion. There are no happenstances.

Some people will want to address their spiritual will to family generally, or to a specific family member; others want to speak to friends, or coworkers; some just want to write what they have found important in life; about that which has brought challenge, joy, beauty, suffering, or wisdom to their lives. The desire, maybe even the drive, is to pass on some of the wisdom of one's experiences to those who come after.

You may want to write primarily to yourself, saying: This is who I am trying to be. This is who I think I am.

What follows are some sample wills but they in no way cover the gamut of possibilities.

You will notice some real differences in the wills of those who are seventy years or older compared to those who are still in the middle of their lives. Those who are older are generally "looking back," while those under seventy are generally looking ahead. All are on a journey, but the younger person does not see or feel the road becoming shorter, or maybe ending sooner. For the middle-agers, there is generally no end in sight yet. Those who are younger are beginning to focus on what is most important, and beginning to choose a more defined purpose for their lives. Those who are older want to share what they've learned, and what's most precious for passing on.

Sample Will #1

The author of the first sample spiritual will is a fifty-seven-year-old woman, a friend of mine, who is a convert to Catholicism. She tells part of her own inspirational story and concludes with a challenge to herself. (This is a great thing to do—make a challenge to yourself in your will.)

She has struggled to deal with anxiety and fear in some of the challenges and circumstances in her life. I suspect that she will revisit this will every several years, and rewrite it when she is ready to ponder what legacy she wishes to leave. She'll measure herself and her progress with the help of good friends, or perhaps her priest or a spiritual director. She's on a journey, a spiritual journey that never ends! She begins:

> Words I try to live by:
> "Therefore I tell you, do not worry about your life, what you will eat or what you will drink, or about your body, what you will wear. Is not life more than food, and

the body more than clothing? Look at the birds in the sky: they do not sow nor reap, they gather nothing into barns, yet your heavenly Father feeds them. Are you not more important than they?" (Mt 6:25–26).

It is so comforting to read the above verses about God's love and God's promise to take care of us. Yet, I have been living in anxiety and fear. I have been trying to control every aspect of my life because I am not wise and my faith is weak. Looking back, there is not much comfort in events that I willed to happen, but I am in awe of God's miracles in my life. Letting go is a challenge I have been working on and I hope my children will realize the importance of letting go sooner than I did.

When my family was living in Beijing, China, in 2003, we went to Sunday Mass at the Canadian Embassy presided over by an American Franciscan priest. I cherished the emails of support and encouragement he sent to my husband and me when we were going through a difficult time in our lives.

I learned that I had Myelodysplastic Syndrome the same day I found out I was pregnant with my third child. The doctor called me at home to tell me that my blood test result was terribly abnormal and I had to go back to the hospital the next day. I went back every day for two weeks until I was finally diagnosed. My best friend from college who was a hematology oncologist in Florida told me to come back to the United States. She could not believe that I had a disease that is most common among men over sixty-five. After introducing me to a few transplant doctors who told me the odds of survival were thirty percent at best, my friend found me a National Institute of Health protocol for a sibling stem cell transplant. The venerable doctor was achieving a seventy-five percent success rate. I have a younger brother and sister and each had twenty-five percent chance of a match. My sister, my mom's third child, whom my mother did not want to have for economic reasons and had unsuccessfully deployed an old-wives'-tale method to abort, was a match. Miracle number one!

Then came the hard part. My doctor said to me, "Look me in my eyes. You have two little children in the waiting room who need their mother. You have to terminate your pregnancy and get better right now." We tried to terminate three times but each time it was thwarted. Then my doctor relented and told me to try carrying the baby as long as my blood level was stable. It was risky but he also thought it would be better for my emotional well-being to keep the baby that I had genuinely wanted after two miscarriages. The second miracle no one expected was that my blood level improved as pregnancy progressed. I was able to give birth to a healthy boy at thirty-eight weeks.

Our priest was so happy for us. But then I faced the formidable task of getting the stem cell transplant. I expressed my anxiety to Father over whether I could survive this and if not, what will happen to the newborn baby. He was rightly disappointed in me for having such little faith. God had brought me this far and I was stressing over what would happen next. Father said life is much more fun if I let God take charge and "go for the ride." I wish I still had his wise emails.

Last week, we celebrated my youngest son's thirteenth birthday. God has been so good to me and my family despite my still fretting over everything. But last year my sister said, "I don't know how it is so easy for you to just go with the flow." I guess I am making some progress. God showed me repeatedly who was in charge and that he is full of love and goodness. I still have a long way to go but I am trying.

—Connie Chung Schramm, age fifty-seven

Many contemplating writing a will may be inspired, or find insight into their lives, through the reading and reflection on a scripture passage, or a poem, a writing from the classics, the philosophers, old and recent, or a spiritual leader, Catholic or not (I love Rumi, Hafiz, and many other Eastern writers, too).

Those who choose in midlife to think about writing a spiritual will and begin journaling, either writing in a notebook or digitally, may want to use reflections on scripture passages, or classic writings, as inspiration each day. They can serve as seeds that will be the beginnings of the spiritual will.

Sample Will #2

This next spiritual will conveys what I would call strong "generational" values—it is the sort that is usually written by someone who feels they are approaching the end of their life. As you will notice, at least by the end of this sample, it is written by me!

> Dear Nieces and Nephews:
>
> I have thought much about what I want to leave you that is not something you can touch, (those were left to you in my legal will), but these are things you may recall only through your memory. These "gifts" may conjure up pictures in your mind's eye, or bring one of your senses into play: sight, smell, and even touch.
>
> What I wish to pass on are my values, which I inherited from my mother and father, your grandparents. They were learned more through sight and presence than with words, and I find now, after these many years, those virtues have been important for me to emulate and have become part of my DNA. (You may well find them also to be part

of yours; I have already witnessed them in you.) Only let them grow in you and pass them on! They make the world a better place in which to live.

My dad was a man of integrity, who cared deeply for his family, his church, his business, and his employees. Justice, charity, and gratitude were words that defined him to me and to so many others. At tax time, he would say, "I am so happy to pay my taxes. This country has been so good to me." I haven't heard that in ages! Loving the country that has given you so many opportunities is important but doesn't mean that one cannot speak up when the values which we hold are not upheld in our leaders or by our government.

My dad wasn't perfect! For example, he smoked too many cigars. Whenever I smell cigar smoke today, I still become nostalgic and tears can still form in my eyes at the aroma. Cigar smoke meant that Dad was home! And that meant security and warmth. So did sights and smells, food and cooking, coffee brewing, and apple pie baking—all important aspects of a happy household. I experienced all of these in my youth and have continued into old age to relish and applaud them.

Hospitality was a hallmark of our house. Your grandparents welcomed family, friends, parishioners, priests, all who came. Dad was a wonderful cook and having food and drink for all guests was very important to both Mom and Dad. Now, I continue to welcome all who come to our house. Hospitality is such a wonderful gift, even though it is demanding. There is such richness in meeting and sharing around the table.

There was always laughter in our house growing up. I inherited it well and am frequently told, "When you are in the house, there is laughter."

I pray that *joy* will always be part of your life. No one feels joy all of the time, but a deep faith upholds you in the darker times of your life. I have experienced it and pray for that for you. Feeding your faith is as important as feeding your body.

My vision has always been a broad one and entering a religious missionary institute has reinforced that view. The whole world is our home because we are all brothers and sisters under one God. We have much to learn from everyone, from each nation, and each person from any continent, island, or country. I have a firm belief in respect for everyone and the equality of all persons.

While I do not want to preach, I want you to remember me and maybe you will be moved to live out some of the values we have inherited from our past generations. *Do* update them, but with the same faith, love, and spirit.

—Your Aunt Mary Petrosky, F.M.M., age eighty-five

Of course, there are as many ways of writing a spiritual will as there are people on this planet! There is no "right" or "wrong" in this. What is important is that the will comes from the core of the person doing the writing, and then it will be transparent to those who truly know you.

Sample Will #3

This spiritual will was written by an older woman. As you will hopefully do in your own will, this person makes a general listing of what she wishes to leave friends and family when her life comes to an end. It is heartwarming and obviously deeply felt.

What I want to leave to my friends and family:

Believe . . .

- that the mercy of God is inexhaustible.

- that to belong you only have to return over and over to the place you yearn to belong to.
- that a lot of life's difficulties can be avoided by reading the book of Proverbs.
- that the presence of a loving God is seen in how I welcome and love others.
- that when life is overwhelming, pray the Psalms.
- that you should share your life experience with others and listen to theirs.
- that God is always on the phone but you have to pick up the call.
- that Jesus is trying to help you, not judge you. In the Gospel, he is trying to help you live the best way possible.
- that laughing cures a lot.
- that in creating something—cooking, writing, painting, making jokes, dancing, making love, visiting, holding hands, walking the dog—you find your real self.

    And please smile a lot. The world needs it.

    —Linda Baltzer, age sixty-nine

When Linda comes to the end of her life—God willing, years from now—may her loved ones confirm that she indeed left behind these things by the way she spent her time on earth.

You can do the same for those you love.

Sample Will #4

A will similar to the one you just read by Linda in Sample #3 was written by another older woman. She, too, summarizes what she has learned and what she hopes to leave for others. She writes:

I have no children but I do have a rich bounty of nieces and nephews and friends who have enriched my life. For them, when I leave this bright orb, I hope they will remember me fondly and enjoy the gifts I wish to pass on:

Inquisitiveness. Learn all you can about this great world, the people and all the creatures who inhabit it. You cannot possibly be bored and inquisitive at the same time.

Perseverance. No matter what happens, the good, the bad, the unfair, the unreal, the unjust—lay little blame, least of all on yourself. Just keep on going and learn from what transpires.

Travel. Leave your comfort zone periodically and listen to other ideas in other languages, watch different sunsets, see other mountains, eat different foods. All of this will enrich you. Trust me.

Dream. First, discover your dream. Then, pursue it with all your might. Be true to your dream, but if it somehow fails you, still cherish the fact that you had one at all.

Work. Find some occupation that you love and that has meaning for you. Hopefully, you will be of service to the world. This will add great value to your life and keep you happy for a long time.

Regrets. Humans are wired for some mistakes and failures, but use them as lessons. And weigh them against your successes. Then let them go.

Finally, *love.* It is the foundation for life. We were born for love. If lucky, we are loved early and often and learn to love back—people, pets, teachers, food, images, places, things, and ideas. If we get sick, we love health. If we get rich or poor, we love gratitude. And if we stumble in fear or doubt, we love kindness, friendship, and God in all forms.

> This is what I bequeath to you along with this heart-
> felt wish: give life your best shot and always be good to one
> another. We're all we have on earth!
> —Margaret Mary McGovern, age seventy-five

Margaret Mary covers almost all of the ten principles that can enrich one's thinking about the material, content, and ideas that form the basis of a powerful spiritual will.

Her love for her nieces and nephews and friends is evident in all of the areas of life that she names. She has traveled and experienced much of the beauty of God's creation, acknowledging the richness of otherness, as well as an innate kinship through a common humanity. What a fine example!

Sample Will #5

Now, it is time to look at a sample spiritual will from someone in the heart of midlife.

The author of this developing will, Andy, is a civil rights attorney in his forties. He is married and has two young sons. Andy has clearly chosen a focus for his life through his professional experiences, and he is looking to grow as a man, a husband, and a father. This is his first spiritual will, and I'm sure there will be others. As his personal and professional life develops, he will be filling in many more possibilities, hopes, struggles, and insights in the decades to come.

Andy demonstrates by what he writes that he is bringing the insights of the Church and his own study of the scriptures to bear on his professional life.

> I have been offended by bullying for as long as I can remem-
> ber. There is something uniquely ugly to me about watching,

or being victimized by, someone inclined to exploit a power differential for no good reason. As a parent of two small boys, I am especially mindful of the importance of encouraging kindness, respect, and fair play.

Perhaps ironically, as a civil rights attorney, I am regularly called upon to confront bullying, with an eye toward "winning," at least within the context of litigation. But the example set by Jesus challenges me to look beyond the four walls of the courthouse in defining victory. Jesus set the bar higher than just "winning" for ourselves, instructing us to love our enemies and pray for those who persecute us. To paraphrase Martin Luther King Jr., it is not enough to simply win. In winning, we must strive to so appeal to the hearts and consciences of those who oppose us, that we win them too.

Yet it must be emphasized that the Jesus' way is not the way of the doormat. To the contrary, when Jesus was slapped in the face by a guard of the High Priest, he confronted the bully and demanded an explanation: "'I have spoken publicly to the world, I have always taught in a synagogue or in the temple area where all the Jews gather, and in secret I have said nothing.' . . . When he said this, one of the temple guards standing there struck Jesus and said, 'Is this the way you answer the high priest?' Jesus answered him, 'If I have spoken wrongly, testify to the wrong; but if I have spoken rightly, why do you strike me?'" (Jn 18:20–23). A close reading of Jesus famous "turn the other cheek" passage likewise reveals a Jesus who is anything but passive in the face of bullying. Yes, Jesus advised that "when someone strikes you on your right cheek, turn the other one to him as well" (Mt 5:39). But as the late biblical scholar Walter Wink observed, Jesus lived in a largely right-handed world. Therefore, those doing the hitting would typically have used their right hands. Yet the only way to strike someone on the right cheek with one's right hand is a backhanded slap—a gesture typically reserved for an insult or reprimand to those of lesser power and status (e.g., masters to slaves, Romans to Jews). In such a context, turning the "other cheek" represents an act of principled confrontation—challenging the bully to hit the left cheek, but in so doing, forcing him to acknowledge his victim's common humanity.

When I leave this earth, my deepest, most audacious hope, is to leave behind a world not only more inclined to confront bullying but to do so with active, creative, and non-violent methods—ones aimed not just at amplifying our common humanity but the awesome power of God's love.

—Andy Hoffman, age forty-six

Andy is well on his way, focusing on this particular topic of bullying. He shows a passion for his work and his particular field. He is already looking at the "big picture." He has chosen his mentor, Jesus, and studies the scriptures often. He will be adding to this regularly as he reviews and reflects on his growing insights into the value of his profession and his possible contributions to it during his life. Already Andy has recognized that God's love is what he wants to be always his motivation.

Sample Will #6

In the next sample, a woman shares her long spiritual legacy. This will has two distinct but very important parts. The first part deals with her faith and explains the way she lives that faith through a pervading love of the earth—something deeply ingrained in her from growing up in a rural community.

> As I think about my spiritual legacy and what to "will" or "bequeath" to my family and friends, these come to me as most important:
>
> - Faith in God, the Trinity; a God who is personal and personable.
> - Belief in the value of our church's sacramental life.
> - Belief in and devotion to Mary the Mother of God.
> - Belief in the value of teaching, mentoring, and listening to others.
> - Belief in the dignity and goodness of all of creation. Specifically, all of creation must be revered and cared for.
> - Belief in the dignity of each human being. Every person deserves respect, food, shelter, clothing, meaningful work, and a living wage.
> - Belief in life eternal with God, a God who is all-forgiving and merciful, a God who takes us home at the time of death. As St. Mechtilde of Magdeburg said, one's soul returns to God as a needle to a magnet!
> - Belief that the death of the body is just the beginning of a great, new adventure into new life, life which is changed for the better!
>
> And then there is what I do *not* want to leave behind: unfinished business, such as:
>
> - There is an essential need to forgive—to let go—not to carry grudges.

- Reconciliation is essential with family, friends, associates, even if forgiveness is not accepted.

An important aspect of my legacy follows.

I love nature. And I love gardening. I see the divine hand at work, spinning, weaving, shaping all of nature's glory! We read in the book of Genesis how God divided the waters of chaos to form the dry land, thus making "the earth," and the waters to be "the sea"—abundant and life-giving. Then God said that every sort of seed-bearing plant and fruit-bearing tree should come forth. They did and it was all good. From this same good earth, God forms us again and again, in the divine image.

Surely our God loves the earth, the ground, the soil. Every nation on earth shows endless examples of the divine, reveling in the land. There are trees to stabilize the hills, to protect the shores, to hold birds' nests, and children's swings. There are plants to filter the water, to give us food and medicine, and flowers to smell. Some seem given mostly to praise and reflect God's greatness in their endless varieties, sizes, colors, fragrances, and ability to adapt. This is our earth! What must heaven be like?

My genes for digging and planting come from our Austrian, German, and Irish ancestors, hardy farmers all of them. While they farmed for their livelihood, I have been blessed to be able to do it for the sheer enjoyment of it. I find working in the soil—planting, weeding, watering, and mulching—to be relaxing, stimulating, creative, and so therapeutic and healing.

Jesus got down in the dirt, too. He spat on the ground and made clay from the soil to heal a blind person. When he forgave and healed the woman caught in adultery, he first bent down and wrote in the dirt. When he arose in loving compassion for her did he put his hand on her head? Did he touch her on the forehead, leaving a bit a dust there? Reminds me of Ash Wednesday! And this brings me back to remembering that we are dust and how good that dust was, is, and will always be . . . so good that the product of the fields and the fruit of the vine were chosen to be our sacramental bread and wine—Jesus Christ himself!

Truly, I wish to promote a love for the earth that nourishes, protects, and delights us as a loving mother and father, love for the earth in which we can play and create new things.

I will do this by:

- Purchasing as much as possible locally grown foods to support farmers.
- Consuming less, recycling, and re-purposing consumer goods more.
- Supporting, philosophically and financially, environmental groups that work to protect our planet—soil, water, and air—from waste and pollution.
- Supporting ecologically sound legislation.
- Praying in thanks to the most high Lord for our beautiful earth and universe.

—Mary V. Widhalm, age seventy-eight

Mary's love of the earth and all that it has meant in her life is a gift she would like to pass on to others. You can see many of the ten principles played out in her will. She also introduces the need for forgiveness, to attempt to reach equanimity with all, to live in peace with oneself and the world. These are essential features in spiritual wills that aim not just to leave something behind for others but to be instruments of faith, hope, and healing in their own right.

Sample Will #7

This next sample demonstrates that a spiritual will can be very personal and individual. Sometimes our personal story is essential to what we hope to convey. That is definitely the case in this spiritual will, written by an old friend of mine, and a fellow Franciscan religious sister, born and raised in Spain. It communicates strong religious, cultural, and spiritual values that she wants to pass on. I am grateful and humbled that she has allowed me to share it with you.

> My dear family,
>
> It is the custom in our society, as we near the end of our lives, to draw up a Will or Testament of financial goods that one possesses—for the benefit of family members, friends, or different charitable societies, according to each case. Well, since by the grace of God, I have already had a long life with health and without great infirmities, this has allowed me to remain active up to the present moment. Nevertheless, being a religious, I cannot leave a financial legacy to my family, but instead, one that is spiritual.
>
> I wish to go back to the fifties to begin my account that none of you know, since I have never shared this with you. I believe that I was a happy young person in the heart of a united Christian family, with a mother who was good, caring, and joyful, and a father who was a good provider. Those were difficult times because Spain was emerging from a cruel civil war.
>
> I was the typical young Spanish woman, conceited and flirtatious. I frequented the movies, places for young people, and beaches in the summer, with my dear sisters and good friends. But we were also devout young people,

going to daily Mass, who dedicated part of our days to apostolic works, in the Legion of Mary, Daughters of Mary, spiritual retreats, and other causes.

All this was on the surface because within my heart was "another song." One fine day, when I was seventeen years old, I felt, I heard, that God was calling me for him to religious life, to the missions, to make Jesus known to those who did not know him. My first impulse was *no*, why me?

I tried at all cost to quench the Voice that was calling me. It is difficult to express about the Voice. Within, very much within one's being, the Voice speaks to a person, calls him or her, insists and insists. . . . How to turn it off? There is no way. How could I separate myself from my family, my parents, my brother and sisters, friends, suitors? Life was good and I was having fun. However, I could not stop thinking that God wanted me for himself because God continued to call me through that Voice within.

I lost the battle. Because of such insistence, I had to give up and surrender myself. From that moment, my life was one of great anguish, and with alarm I counted the days remaining for me in my family. I did not have the strength to leave everything, but God was my strength and it is he who led me by his hand and carried me. I will never forget the day I left home. I had such a large knot in my throat that I couldn't speak. Before leaving home with my parents, I went from one bed to another to kiss my brother and sisters. I knew they were awake, but no one moved; I think they were crying. During the trip from Bilbao to Pamplona tears were sliding down my cheeks without my being able to hold them back. Not one of the three of us pronounced one word during the journey.

Ah! But God is good. And as soon as I entered the novitiate, I knew that I was in the right place, and I was inundated with peace and spiritual well-being. That is not to say that I didn't have to confront my little battles, one after another, because of the desire to return to my family. I missed them so much. But again, God was my strength who held me by his hand and walked with me.

A year and a half after my entrance to the novitiate I was transferred to the novitiate of Grottaferrata, near Rome. Another great break. Another sad farewell to my beloved Spain, and four years later I would have to say goodbye again to leave Europe and go to the United States. My mission.

I believe you know that the Franciscan Missionaries of Mary are dedicated to both missionary work and adoration of the Blessed Sacrament. We make at least half an hour of Adoration every day before the Blessed Sacrament and during this half hour it is God and me alone. From the first day that I entered the convent and went on my knees before the Blessed Sacrament, I have petitioned God for each one of you. I have named you one by one and as the years passed the list began to grow and continues growing, but God listens to all your names every day. I also know how to be persistent, just like God. And I have been so for more than sixty years.

My petition for all is my legacy: I ask God to keep you, to bless you, to guide you, to strengthen you in times of trial, to increase your faith, so that nothing can make you ashamed of being a Christian. May you be among those who make a difference in this world. When you help and give a hand to the needy, may you see God in the face of the other because God is creator of us all. In a word, may you always live with your gaze upon our God who has created us for himself and one day will call us again to himself, and

may the most Blessed Mary also guide your steps united to
her Son, Our Lord Jesus Christ.
>   —Always united in Jesus and Mary,
>   María Teresa de los Ríos, F.M.M., age eighty-five

Sr. María Teresa sent this to her family members who were deeply
moved. It strengthened their already strong family bonds. This letter
is a good example of both the first principle, which emphasizes the
importance of writing from love, and the tenth principle, reminding
us of the belief in the eternal relationships we hold with our belief in
the Communion of Saints.

Sr. María Teresa's will is also a fine example of telling a personal
story in a way that will inspire those who know and love us. I'm sure
that some of her family had never heard all of this about her, and they
are probably delighted, now, not only to know, but to have this in hand.

Sample Will #8

Peter is in his mid-fifties. He has been a public school teacher for
many years and is presently tutoring individual students. He has
been a member of AA for some time. From his own struggles with
alcohol, he writes of what he wants to leave to those to whom he
will eventually address a final version of this developing spiritual
will. He writes:

> I would very much like to leave to the sick and suffering,
> lost, and/or confused young adult, a direction I had been
> given that if taken could potentially save their lives and
> definitely save them a lot of time and energy.
>
> It has been my personal experience that when I am
> focused on myself I fall into despair. Concentrating on my

needs and wants, aches and pains, hopes and dreams, or comparing myself with others, leaves me in a place of always falling short and feeling sorry for myself. I can become so preoccupied obsessing on "self" that I am not appreciative or grateful for everything given to me in the present moment—all the abundance around me and the blessings I've been given.

I was victimizing myself this way and became filled with discomfort, spiritually empty, anxious and physically sick. I lashed out at the world in a constant state of "fight or flight," attempting to fill the emptiness with alcohol and cigarettes. Unfortunately, this was my natural way of living for a very long time. It eventually brought me to my knees, broken and asking God for help. I told God I was sick and tired of being sick and tired. God did help me. On that day, God spoke to me through a passage in Isaiah 40:30–31:

> Though young men faint and grow weary, and youths
>   stagger and fall,
> They that hope in the Lord will renew their strength.

It was only after finding AA that it became evident to me that to "hope in Yahweh" is to attempt to understand what God wants for me every moment of every day. In my simple attempt to understand God's will as often as possible, I open a door to action and a life beyond my wildest dreams.

Seeking out God's will for my life has given me a relationship with the Holy Spirit as well as countless blessings. While I'm doing the will of my Higher Power, I am strengthened physically and given a clear sense of direction. After I do "the next right action," as they say in AA, I feel energized and a part of God's presence through my community: a worker among workers. I can now say that God is in each and every one of us, ever reminding us how much we are loved. Matthew 22:37–40 reads: "You shall love the Lord, your God, with all your heart, with all your soul, and with all your mind. This is the greatest and the first commandment. The second is like it: You shall love your neighbor as yourself. The whole law and the prophets depend on these two commandments."

—Peter Cohen, age fifty-five

Peter addresses these beginning words of a possible developing will to the "sick and suffering, lost, and/or confused" young adult, and offers a direction to them as well as to others with similar challenges. As the years pass, undoubtedly, he will be adding some new insights into what life has been teaching him. He has based much of his narrative on many of the principles of Alcoholics Anonymous, as well as on emphasizing the necessity of love. He writes honestly, genuinely, and almost transparently of his own struggles and failures. He is already preparing to name what he would like to leave to others based on his own experiences in life—and I suspect that he will turn to his document again and again to remind himself of the principles he holds most dear.

Sample Will #9

Lori is a mother of two young boys and the editor of a magazine. She is married to Andy, and together they are seeking, as a family, to live out their values in service to others and to the world which they inhabit, at work, at home, in their local community, and in their church. She writes:

In the Gospel of Mark, Jesus tells us to love our neighbor as our self. And many times over he forgave sinners not by shaming or feeling sorry for them but by understanding where they've been. And by taking the form of a man, Jesus embodied the ultimate expression of empathy. He literally put himself in our shoes—to feel as we feel. How wonderful would it be, in this increasingly divisive world that we live in, to receive God's gift of empathy and share it as often as possible? It is at the core of my spiritual life, and I believe it can be taught and deepened through practice.

When I was very young, my parents would occasionally argue (whose parents don't?). While I never really knew what it was that was causing tension, I could see the way my parents both reacted. My mother, who wore her emotions on her sleeve, would weep and retreat to the bedroom. My sister and brother would often join her for comfort. As much as I felt the pull of that bedroom, I felt my place needed to be in the living room, where my dad would be sitting quietly. I knew that although he was less transparent about his feelings, he too was suffering, and I didn't want him to be alone. It was then that I first began to understand the beauty that depth and empathy can bring to our relationships.

Now that I am older, there are very few interactions that I have in my day where I don't feel either compelled or challenged to empathize—by the stranger on the subway who is angrily elbowing into the crowd, the insecure coworker who needs constant praise, the babysitter who is late again and again. And as a mother raising two young boys in an age where more value is often placed on digital interactions than on human connection, I realize now more than ever how important it is to model this behavior for my children. Sometimes it's enough to sympathize, to feel sad for a friend who is grieving or say a prayer for a homeless man who is sleeping in the alcove of a storefront. But I want to instill in my children the gift of empathy, whereby they try to feel the grief of that friend and offer the kind of words they would want offered to themselves; or try to imagine the painful life journey one might take to homelessness. It is in these moments of understanding that we forge closer bonds with each other or bridge what sometimes seem like cavernous divides.

—Lori Hoffman, age forty-five

Lori has discovered early the need for, and the value and beauty of, empathy. She has already chosen to focus on empathy in her work life, family life, and generally throughout all aspects of her encounters with others. Her developing spiritual will reveals that she is a sensitive woman, recognizing others' feelings and needs.

I am sure that as the years pass, Lori will continue to model and deepen the values evident in what she's already written. It will be interesting to see when she writes the final copy of her spiritual will, how this gift of empathy may have matured and deepened. She may then share what the living out of her gift has taught her and is worth passing on to others.

Sample Will #10

This last sample will is written by Jack, an older gentleman who has been struggling with many medical issues which have left him somewhat limited in his activities and energy level. He remains in his apartment with his wife. His medications leave him rather lethargic and in need of additional sleep throughout the day. Jack obviously has been reflecting much on his whole life, both his professional work in family court and volunteer ministries.

One day as I was working as an intake officer in family court, I looked out at a crowded waiting room and called for my next client. An elderly African-American woman stood up, picked up her packages and came to the door where I waited. She looked up, saw me and said, "Thank God it is you!" I thanked her and replied, "May I ask why you say that?" The woman answered, "Because you are so kind." Obviously, I felt happy and even more so because I did not remember having met this woman before.

A few years later at my retirement party a young probation officer said to me, "I hope to do what you did . . . to remain a caring person without having a heart attack or getting shot!"

"You are so kind." "You are a caring person." If this is true, it is because I believe that every human being has a dignity. In addition, because of my Christian faith I believe that every human being has a destiny: eternal life. It can be very difficult to accept these truths and sometimes even more difficult to live by them. Why? Because actions speak louder than words.

A few years ago, I volunteered at a Sunday afternoon soup kitchen conducted by the Jesuit fathers at St. Francis Xavier Church in New York City. More than one thousand guests were served a hot meal. Obviously, many volunteers were needed to make this happen. In all honesty, I was trying to find a comfortable way to end my volunteering at this site. I found everything wonderful except the fact that all present, volunteers and guests, used the same bathrooms. There were often unpleasant disturbances in the bathrooms. However, one volunteer made me evaluate the depth of my commitment to the human dignity of all people. Let us say his name was Alan. He was said to have volunteered at St. Francis every Sunday for almost nine years. No one ever knew him to miss a Sunday. One day in Father's absence, Alan asked me to lead the community in prayer before our meal. I told him I would be honored to have him lead the prayer. He replied, "But I don't believe in God."

I emphasize that this is a true story. That day I met a man who believed in the dignity of all human beings and acted upon that belief.

Belief in human dignity is a matter of philosophical and/or religious belief. Once again my volunteer work proved to me how difficult it can be to believe in basic religious truths. One struggles to believe in a good God when one has seen the work of the Hitlers of the world. I met a Jewish woman in a nursing home who, with her husband, had fled Hitler's Nazis. They fled across Europe and to the United States. Her husband died here. They did not have children. When I started visiting her each week, though, I was in awe of her knowledge of history and of her humility. We never spoke of religion, until one day when I found her wearing an oxygen cannula. Her heart was in difficulty. From out of nowhere she asked, "Jack, do you think people are better off as they approach death if during life they had some kind of religious faith?" We talked for a while and I asked if she would like to see a chaplain. She said yes, and I made the referral. She died two days later. Again, an absolutely true story.

I personally have come to believe in the dignity of all and of a God who is good and who cares. Why? Good question.

The value of the struggle to have faith and to act on that faith is a belief worth handing on. As I am now retired and enduring some health problems, I have no plans to join any more volunteer groups. However, as I have done in the past, I will try to accept any invitation to speak about or write about my belief in human dignity. I have done this in the past and perhaps my history of some success and much failure will inspire others to keep on trying.

—Jack Gerrity, age eighty-two

Spending time facing and undergoing treatment for serious maladies, Jack is using his quiet, reflective time to review his life. He is recalling and then recognizing what he did that was of particular value over his many decades of experience. He has accomplished many marvelous things in his work and in his volunteer ministries with the homeless and with nursing home patients. But now he has come to recognize that some of the most important actions of his life were those moments when a person he encountered recognized and acknowledged the significance of his respect for their individual dignity. His attitude and action could only have come from the core of his being which is based on his deep beliefs that God is *good*, God is *love*, and that each individual he encountered was a gift.

There is great variety in these ten sample spiritual wills, both in content and in style. Each person, accepting the invitation to contribute a sample, wrote freely and enthusiastically. While each commented that he or she had never heard of writing such a will, they each recognized its value immediately. In fact, this book was only in process while these ten people, wrote their spiritual wills. Each was given a brief explanation of what a spiritual will could be, and what it was not. They are all people with whom I am now working on this process for deepening their engagement with life. Five of the wills were written by people seventy years and older; five were written by those under seventy. Those who are younger are looking forward, while the older writers tend to be looking backward. That's perfectly normal! But all are certainly looking inward and outward.

You may have noticed the great variety in each of the wills. Some are very short, naming succinctly what the person is leaving to the ones to whom the will is directed. Some are merely a summary of suggestions for surviving, enduring, conquering obstacles, supporting others, and enjoying what life offers. Some are longer and some are very personal letters, addressed to family members. These tend to express more emotion and affection. Other wills are more detailed, not just naming the developing "gifts" but giving the "whys" and "hows" that come with naming those gifts which they wish to leave behind for others.

Some articulate the motivation that brought them to their choices, whether a scripture reading or a spiritual insight. For some, there is a focus in their professional life related to a deeper spiritual longing; they have begun an in-depth search for meaning in their lives and have begun to put that down on paper (or pixels). What begins as a professional focus, by choice or happenstance, may well develop into not only a work commitment but into distinct spiritual values and goals. As we learn to bring the two together the older we become, we grow into a calling, more than a career. It is most often from such a calling, and the person's response to it, that the material in a spiritual will is born.

Each will reflects the personality of the writer in a unique way. It comes from his or her body, soul, and spirit. Ideally, each spiritual testament should be as free as the Spirit who inspired the writer.

This book is about a journey that never ends; that journey begins at birth, but begins in earnest when we begin to establish, and live by, the principles and values that will guide our lives. The spiritual culmination of this journey can be the way each writer sees value in his or her life, and commits to passing it on to future generations.

You will remember that this book began with my review of the four questions with which my philosophy teacher challenged me in my first philosophy class many years ago. I recently recalled an experience in Papua New Guinea, as a young missionary in the 1970s. While giving a retreat to the sisters of a recently founded local community, one retreatant described herself to me in pidgin English as "*mi meri belong graun*." Translated, this means, "I am a woman of the earth." Oh, how that simple but profound answer taught me much and challenged me to grow! This woman had simply answered the first basic question, "Who am I?" Her answer, however, became an occasion of contemplation and gratitude to God as I recalled it later.

A spiritual will can teach, or, remind you, of many such epiphanies in your life. The time you spend writing what you want to include will elicit your own memories of how you discovered answers to those four questions, and others that may occur to you. The answers are the treasures of your journey which you want to leave for others because—believe me—the journey never ends.

St. Francis of Assisi is one of the most well-known and loved saints in the Catholic Church and throughout the world. In his biography about St. Francis, St. Bonaventure reported that Francis told his spiritual brothers—his fellow Friars Minor—before he died: "I have done what was mine to do, may Christ teach you what is yours."

I couldn't ever say it better than that.

Chapter 5
WRITING YOUR SPIRITUAL WILL

Now we really begin. Previous chapters have prepared you to begin answering the basic questions of the spiritual will, including those four original ones that challenged me those many years ago. You might add a fifth question: What do I leave behind? The answers to these questions, and some of your own, should prompt you to take your life seriously and reverently as a gift which has something in it, not just for you, but for others.

You should now be ready.

If not, recall the ten principles that we outlined previously. Summarizing them, I would say:

An effective spiritual will is written out of *love*. It might be love for family, for friends, for all aspects of creation, for a particular love or a particular interest of the person writing the will. Love is the grounding and heart of the spiritual will. It may begin with God or with something in his Word, the wisdom of the ancients, both east and west, or the beauty in this universe.

To be believable, the will must be honest, genuine, and transparent.

The will may include your dreams and hopes, realized or not. It is important to include also the reasons you aimed for your personal dreams and the energy that you used to attain them, with reasons why they succeeded or failed.

All of your experiences—relationships, family, education, and travels at home or abroad—will feed your writing. What you have found beautiful in the world, in the arts, in music, and in peoples everywhere will also be relevant, along with your contacts with other countries, cultures, races, foods, customs, beliefs, and climes. If you believe in the Communion of Saints, or another expression of that communion, writing a spiritual will can be seen as an expression of that belief. You, in the here and now, are united through the generations preceding you and to those following you by this simple act of writing a spiritual will.[11]

My Spiritual Will

Written by

_____

On this day

_____

Witnessed by, or presented to:

_____

and

_____

I. BASIC THINGS YOU SHOULD KNOW ABOUT ME

Who you are.

I am . . .

_____

_____

_____

_____

Where you come from.

I come from . . .

_____

_____

_____

_____

Here are some additional questions to help you focus in on who you are, and how you became the person you are. Answer any or all of them, inasmuch as they help you to consider what you want to leave to others.

1. What gets me out of bed in the morning?

_____

_____

2. What is my passion?

_____

_____

3. What would I be willing to die for?

_____

_____

4. What gives me a sense of awe—such as a sunrise, a sunset, the beauty of fall leaves, my favorite season? What has frightened me—in nature, a storm at sea, a plane ride with turbulence, almost drowning, driving in a blizzard, the uncertainty of earthquakes, the threat of terrorism, etc.?

_____

_____

5. What experience of beauty—such as a work of art or a piece of music—has moved me, lifted me out of myself?

_____

_____

6. What is my favorite season? Why do I like it so much?

_____

_____

7. What gives me a feeling of security: a person, a smell, a touch, a sight, a place?

_____

_____

8. Have I had what I would call a spiritual experience, or an experience of being in the presence of God? *These experiences might be both joyful and scary.*

_____

_____

9. What do I dream about that gives me joy or peace?

_____

_____

10. Where do I find peace, inner peace? *Describe a setting, a place, where you are the most comfortable.*

_____

_____

11. Do I have a favorite sport, a favorite place, a favorite animal, a favorite food, a favorite country or culture? Why do I like it so much? What has it taught me?

_____

_____

12. How do I handle disappointment, failure, success?

_____

_____

13. What relationships have I valued most in life?

_____

_____

14. What relationships have challenged me the most?

_____

_____

II. THERE ARE THINGS I WANT TO SAY

Now, let the words flow. To whom do you need to speak? What do you want to say? Are you speaking primarily to yourself, or to others? Refer back to the examples from pages 23–50 if you need help to get started.

_____

_____

_____

_____

III. WHAT I WANT TO LEAVE BEHIND
WHEN MY LIFE ON EARTH IS OVER

Now, make a list.

What do I want to leave behind for family? From the bottom of my heart, please know:

_____

_____

Their names are:

_____

_____

What do I want to leave to my friends?

_____

_____

Their names are:

_____

_____

What do I want to leave to my colleagues?

_____

_____

Their names are:

_____

_____

IV. MORE

Speak from your heart, here, saying whatever else you need or want to say. What you write will probably all be centered around gently expressing "When you do this, you will be remembering me."

_____

_____

AFTERWORD

As "his health deteriorated and death drew near," Francis of Assisi dictated a final message to his followers that is commonly referred to as his *Testament*. The Franciscan family has placed special value on this document for two reasons. First, it provides a succinct summary of the Poor Man's "wisdom and vision." Put simply, his vision was the "life of the Gospel," to "follow the teaching and footprints of the Lord Jesus Christ."[12] Second, in the *Testament,* Francis reveals the four primary events that clarified his vision, moved his heart, and led him to embrace a Gospel way of life as a lesser brother. The most significant events included being led by grace to "show mercy" to lepers, to become a man of living faith, to welcome the brothers whom the Lord gave him, and how "the Most High himself revealed to me that I should live according to the form of the Gospel."[13]

Francis's *Testament* is, in essence, his spiritual will. It summarizes the key events through which he learned to live the life to which he was called, and articulates the vision that guided him through the blessings, the challenges, the difficulties, and the choices he made.

As a Franciscan, Mary Petrosky, F.M.M., has embraced the wisdom of the tradition inspired by Francis of Assisi. She has lived it in her own way faithfully, joyfully, and over the course of many years. And although she was called to serve in many different roles as spiritual director, friend, and companion, in numerous places around the world, she has always desired to be a sister among and for others. In the many roles in which she has been called to serve, she has walked with many on their spiritual journey as they, like her, sought to discover, to uncover, their true identity; that is, "What a person is before God and nothing more"—a gift reflecting and revealing uniquely God's goodness.[14]

Mary's reflections in this concise volume reveal the heart of a woman of faith who, in the face of life's complexities and challenges, embraced what was hers to do.[15] Many will be grateful for the wisdom she shares and how, in her life and ministry, she seeks to accompany others in discovering who they are and how they are called to love as God has loved humankind and all creation in Christ and through Christ.

F. Edward Coughlin, O.F.M.
President of Siena College

ACKNOWLEDGMENTS

I want to thank my community, the Franciscan Missionaries of Mary, who "completed" my education in so many ways, but primarily deepened me through its charism, especially for a deep devotion and reverence for the Eucharist. The foundress, Mother Mary of the Passion (Helene de Chappotin), advised us that "Jesus in the Eucharist sends us out to the people, and the people send us back to Jesus in the Eucharist." Any knowledge or wisdom I may be accused of possessing was acquired more from the interchange between the people, me, and then prayer and presence before the Eucharist, more than from the various degrees I acquired.

The opportunity to serve God's people in the United States at various locations, as well as in Rome, Australia, and Papua New Guinea, all opened my mind, heart, and soul to the knowledge, understanding, and wisdom of God's people throughout the world.

The Sisters with whom I have shared international community throughout my religious life have taught me what it means to be a "sister" to all with love and respect, regardless of their language, customs, food, or culture.

To Thomas Lynch, whom I met at a symposium on the topic of dying, where we were both presenters, I wish to express my gratitude for his belief in me. I also wish to thank Jon Sweeney, my editor, who believed in Tom's recommendation for me to write this book. Jon has been an excellent guide, who gave support and enthusiasm for the struggling, elder, neophyte writer!

I want to thank a dear friend, Mary V. Widhalm, who reviewed every word of my manuscript using her computer skills, her intelligence, and her knowledge.

Last, I thank God for my Franciscan affiliation and heritage. With St. Clare, I also thank God for creating me!

GROUP USE GUIDE

The topic of this book is a very sacred and holy subject: one's self and one's journey. The subject of any spiritual will is not just the person in a photograph, someone's exterior or public persona, but it is a glance into someone's very *soul*. In a spiritual will, people reveal as much or as little as they wish to reveal and share, as a gift for others. Sometimes they find support and enlightenment working in and through a group of others who are doing likewise.

Due to the sacredness of the material to be discussed, the choice of each group member is a very important consideration.

If you have been part of a close group of friends—in a book club, yoga group, lectio divina group, health club group, marriage encounter, a group for spiritual direction—you already might have the feeling and understanding of how an effective and supportive group functions. Or you may wish to create a new group not only to discuss this book but to share the experience. A group of between six to eight people is the best size for this discussion.

Here are some suggestions which can offer a deeper experience as well as assistance if you are going to encounter *The Journey Never Ends* in a group setting:

- You may not want to write your spiritual will while in a group but should still prepare to do so through discussion with others.
- Take meaningful notes, as they will assist you when you begin to write your will.
- Be willing to both share (talk) in the group, and listen well. The purpose of your group discussions is to aid each person in discovering the true self from which their spiritual will may evolve.
- Begin each group meeting with a brief time of silence or prayer.
- Reflect on the reason for the gathering. What has brought you together? Invite people to share on this subject.

The First Gathering

It is important that each member of the group has read the book and feels attracted to writing a spiritual will. Each gathering should end with a prayer, either spontaneous or planned. The first meeting should be a discussion on why this book appealed to each one in the group and then why each chose to gather to discuss it more deeply and personally.

What do you see as its value, both to you *and* to those to whom you want to address your will?

The Second Gathering

Review chapter 5. Discuss each of these questions.

1. What gets you out of bed in the morning?

2. What is your passion?

3. What would you be willing to die for?

4. What gives you a sense of awe—such as a sunrise, a sunset, the beauty of fall leaves, your favorite season?

5.   What frightens you— in nature a storm at sea, a plane ride with turbulence, almost drowning, driving in a blizzard, the uncertainty of earthquakes, the threat of terrorism, etc.?

The Third Gathering

Discuss each of these questions from chapter 5.

1.   What experience of beauty—such as a work of art or a piece of music—has moved you, lifted you out of yourself?

2.   What is your favorite season? Why do you like it so much?

3.   What gives you a feeling of security: a person, a smell, a touch, a sight, a place?

4.   Have you had what you would call a spiritual experience, or an experience of being in the presence of God? (These experiences might be both joyful *and* scary.)

5.   What do you dream about that gives you joy or peace?

The Fourth Gathering

Discuss each of these questions from chapter 5.

1.   Where do you find peace, inner peace. Describe a setting, a place, where you are the most comfortable.

2.   Do you have a favorite sport, a favorite place, a favorite animal, a favorite food, a favorite country or culture? Why do you like it so much? What has it taught you?

3.   How do you handle disappointment, failure, success?

4.   What relationships have you valued most in life?

5.   What relationships have challenged you the most?

You have now discussed many questions, and worked through most of the material for preparing to write a spiritual will.

The Fifth Gathering

Review the ten principles on pages 17–18 and discuss their importance. The group may have already begun writing their spiritual wills and should be encouraged to bring what they have already written for selective sharing.

The Sixth Gathering

At this final gathering each person should contribute whatever he or she is willing to share from their will, as well as discuss the value of this group experience.

NOTES

1. Ancius Boethius, *The Consolation of Philosophy*, trans. David R. Slavitt (Cambridge, MA: Harvard University Press, 2008), Book II, 52–56.

2. Jack Riemer and Nathaniel Stampfer, eds., *Ethical Wills and How to Prepare Them: A Guide to Sharing Your Values from Generation to Generation* (Woodstock, VT: Jewish Lights Publishing, 2015), xiii.

3. See Joan D. Chittister, O.S.B., introduction to *Between Two Souls*, by Mary Lou Kownacki (Grand Rapids: MI: Wm B. Eerdmans, 2004), ix.

4. Edgar Albert Guest, "Myself," public domain, accessed at PoemHunter.com.

5. Thomas Merton, *New Seeds of Contemplation* (New York: New Directions, 2007), 34, 7, 281, 41. These are passages singled out by Sue Monk Kidd in her introduction to this edition of the book, xi–xii.

6. See Robert Barron, *And Now I See: A Theology of Transformation* (New York: Crossroad Publishing, 1998).

7. United States Conference of Catholic Bishops, *General Instruction of the Roman Missal* (Washington, DC: USCCB, 2011), no. 79; cf. *Catechism of the Catholic Church*, 2nd ed. (Vatican City: Libreria Editrice Vaticana; Washington, DC: United States Conference of Catholic Bishops, 1994, 1997), 1354.

8. Marty Haugen, "We Remember," from the collection *With Open Hands* (Chicago: GIA Publications, 1980).

9. Emily Dickinson, "A word made flesh is seldom," *The Poems of Emily Dickinson: Variorum Edition*, ed. Ralph W. Franklin (Cambridge, MA: The Belknap Press of Harvard University Press, 1998).

10. *Final Harvest: Emily Dickinson's Poems*, selected and with an introduction by Thomas H. Johnson (Boston: Back Bay Books, 1964), vii.

11. A PDF and a Word document of this may be downloaded at www.avemariapress.com/myspiritualwill.

12. Francis of Assisi, "The Earlier Rule," in *Francis of Assisi: Early Documents, Vol. 1*, ed. by Regis J. Armstrong, et al. (New York: New City Press, 1999), 63–64.

13. Francis of Assisi, "The Testament," in *Francis of Assisi: Early Documents, Vol. 1*, 124–125.

14. See Francis of Assisi, Admonition XIX, 2, in *Francis of Assisi: Early Documents, Vol. 2*, ed. by Regis J. Armstrong, et al. (New York: New City Press, 1999), 135.

15. See Bonaventure, "The Major Legend of St. Francis," XIV, 3, in *Francis of Assisi: Early Documents, Vol. 2*, 642.

Sr. Mary Petrosky, F.M.M., is a psychiatric social worker and a spiritual director who has served her religious order—the Franciscan Missionaries of Mary—in the United States, Australia, and Papua New Guinea.

She entered the Franciscan Missionaries of Mary community in Providence, Rhode Island, in 1951 and professed first vows in 1954. She earned her bachelor's degree in sociology from Emmanuel College (magna cum laude) in Boston and made her final vows in 1957. She earned a master's degree in psychiatric social work from St. Louis University in 1957 and a master's degree in systematic theology with an emphasis on spiritual direction from the Jesuit School of Theology in 1979.

Petrosky has worked in family and child care in New York City and in Sydney, Australia. She founded a counseling center in Papua New Guinea and taught at Holy Spirit Seminary and Xavier Institute of Missiology. She has served in leadership roles for her order in Australia and Papua New Guinea and was provincial of the US Province. She has been at Holy Name of Jesus Convent in New York City, where she has been involved in spiritual direction and pastoral work, since 2003. She also serves in bereavement ministry at Holy Name of Jesus Catholic Church.

Thomas Lynch is an American poet, essayist, and funeral director. His essay collection, *The Undertaking*, won the American Book Award and was a finalist for the National Book Award.

Br. F. Edward Coughlin, O.F.M., is president of Siena College in Albany, New York.

AVE
Ave Maria Press

Founded in 1865, Ave Maria Press,
a ministry of the Congregation of
Holy Cross, is a Catholic publishing
company that serves the spiritual and
formative needs of the Church and its
schools, institutions, and ministers;
Christian individuals and families; and
others seeking spiritual nourishment.

For a complete listing of titles from

Ave Maria Press

Sorin Books

Forest of Peace

Christian Classics

visit www.avemariapress.com

Ave Maria Press
Notre Dame, IN
A Ministry of the United States Province of Holy Cross